Adrian Bloom's Guide to
SOFT FRUIT

text by Ken Muir

GW01007050

Jarrold Colour Publications, Norwich

Soft fruits can be grown over a very wide range of soils and climatic conditions that are experienced in the United Kingdom. Situations that would be hopeless are those that are directly exposed to salty winds coming off the sea, those that are at a height of 600 ft or more and those where the soils overlie rock or are so shallow that local farmers do not attempt to cultivate them.

Exposure to high winds makes regular satisfactory cropping difficult but in most gardens the effects of these on fruit crops can be overcome by establishment of natural or artificial shelter or both.

A healthy crop of various Soft Fruits

Planning

To assist in planning a fruit garden the weights of fruit that a competent gardener could expect to pick from fully grown bushes are as follows:

Blackberry	Ashton Cross	25 lb
	Bedford Giant	20 lb
	Himalaya Giant	16 lb
Blackcurrant		6 lb
Gooseberry		8 lb
Hybrid berry	Marion	7 lb
	Oregon Thornless	12 lb
	Sunberry	16 lb
	Tayberry	16 lb
	Thornless Boysenberry	14 lb
	Thornless Loganberry	12 lb
Red and white currant		8 lb
Strawberry		1 lb

Bird Protection

The worst pests of bush fruits are marauding blackbirds and other species that eat the ripe fruits, and bullfinches, sparrows and other finches that eat the fruit buds during the winter. To prevent a lesser or greater proportion of the fruit from being lost each year, the only really effective remedy is to erect a fruit cage. This could be either a temporary tubular framework that is covered with a net during the fruit season, or a permanent structure that is covered with wire netting.

The Rotation of Crops

One disadvantage of a permanent fruit cage is that it makes rotation of the various fruit crops difficult. This is not an insuperable difficulty. The first planting of strawberries could be followed by a second bed and by the time the latter had reached the end of its useful life, one of the more permanent crops would be due for grubbing and could change places with the strawberries. Alternatively, after ten or twelve years, a new fruit plot could be planted and the fruit cage transferred to it.

Site

Where there is a choice, a site should be selected that is at the top of any slope exposed to the full sun and not shaded by trees, hedges or walls. The provision of shelter for soft-fruit bushes is most important. On a site with medium exposure to the prevailing winds, average yields can be reduced by twenty per cent, and some years yields can be reduced by as much as forty per cent. For the short term, shelter should be provided by erecting on the windward side a screen of artificial netting that consists of fifty per cent material, so that the wind is slowed down rather than blocked. For the long term, a natural screen such as *Escallonia*, Beech or *Cupressus* should be planted. It should be situated several feet away from the fruit to avoid shading and root competition. A hedge 10 ft high would provide shelter for fruit and other subjects for a distance of 100 ft.

Soils

Fortunately soft fruits produce good crops on a wide range of soils from heavy clays to shallow sands, provided they are given proper care and attention. They grow best on deep soils that provide a large bulk of soil for the roots to exploit and obtain nutrients and water.

Dig the top soil with a spade to a depth of 10–12 in.; any hard pans in the 12 in. below this should be broken with a fork. At the same time, particularly on light soils and gravels, the forking of a heavy application of one barrow load to 6 square yards (10 lb per square yard) of bulky organic matter into the subsoil will improve the soil's fruit-growing quality. The organic matter should be mixed with the soil and not placed in a thick layer at the bottom of the trench.

Heavy soils that have a blue-coloured subsoil should be improved by the placing of a tile drain through the centre of the fruit plot at a depth of 24 in. The drain should be covered with 4 in. of coarse gravel or cinders and empty into a ditch or soakaway.

Perennial Weed Control

Many of the kinds of fruit that are planted have the ability to continue cropping satisfactorily for ten to twenty years if they do not have to compete with perennial weeds. While digging the soil in the manner recommended in the section on soils, the opportunity should be taken to make sure that the roots of any perennial weeds are removed and destroyed. If this cannot be done or the amount of root is too large to deal with in this way, the plot should not be cropped for one summer and should be treated with weedkiller. The perennial weeds that give most trouble among the fruit are common couch, broad leaved dock, ground elder, horsetail and thistle.

The treatment consists (in February) of controlling annual weeds by making an application of one sachet of Weedex (simazine) in 2 gallons of water to 50 square yards with a watering can or spraying machine. This application allows the unrestricted growth of the perennial weeds. When these are fully grown, sometime in June, an application of 2 fl. oz. of Fison's Tumbleweed in 2 gallons of water to 100 square yards should be sprayed on the weeds in the cool of the evening when there is a weather forecast of dry weather for at least twenty-four hours. Great care should be taken to ensure that none of the spray drifts outside the plot as it is likely to kill or severely impair any cultivated plant on which it falls.

The correct application of Tumbleweed should kill over ninety-five per cent of the weeds. Within three to four weeks it should be possible to see any weeds that are not going to die and will require a second application. Finally, dig the plot over in September in preparation for planting.

Growth of annual weeds prevented by application of Weedex *compared with untreated soil*

Liming

Fruit crops grow better and give the heaviest crops when the soil is slightly acid; that is, with a pH of 6.5. It is at this level that all the major and minor plant nutrients will be most readily available to the fruit bushes, and at which added fertiliser will be effectively absorbed by the roots.

The soil from the plot should be tested with a soil testing kit and if it is acid, the appropriate amount of lime that the colour chart indicates should be broadcast over the plot. The lime should be forked into the soil.

Fertiliser Applications

The main requirement by all fruit crops is for potash fertiliser, while their requirement for phosphatic fertiliser is minimal and the application of organic manures such as bone meal is an absolute waste.

A new garden that is being brought into cultivation for the first time should have broadcast over it, after digging:

2 oz. of superphosphate per square yard; 1 oz. of sulphate of potash per square yard.

An established garden that has been under vegetable or fruit production for over five or ten years does not require these additional applications. In both situations, in subsequent pages specific recommendations are made for the application of fertiliser before planting and each subsequent year for each crop.

Raspberry leaves, showing potash deficiency (left) and manganese deficiency (right)

Bulky Organic Manure

If possible, in preparation for planting it is sufficient that one barrowload to 6 square yards (10 lb per square yard) in the form of farmyard manure, spent mushroom manure or garden compost, should be spread on the soil after digging and forked in. Bulky organic matter may be replaced by a quarter of its volume as peat. Poultry manure should not be regarded as an organic manure but as a substitute for fertiliser.

The Purchase of Healthy Planting Stock

The most important reason for soft-fruit crops failing to make satisfactory growth and bear heavy crops is virus diseases. These differ from other kinds of plant diseases in two important ways. Firstly, they are caused by agents too small to be seen even with the aid of an optical microscope. The gardener can only detect viruses by means of symptoms they cause in plants. Secondly, once plants become infected by viruses, they remain infected and all such plants propagated vegetatively by means of suckers, runners and cuttings are themselves infected. Plants growing in the garden cannot be freed from viruses, nor can they be protected by means of chemicals.

The only way to prevent the worst effects of viruses is to purchase healthy plants in the first place in the knowledge that experience has shown that they will crop satisfactorily for a number of years before new virus infections have too serious an effect on growth and yield. Therefore, it is important that plants should be purchased from nurserymen who sell stocks that have been certified by the Ministry of Agriculture as being healthy and true to name. It should be possible to purchase certified plants of blackcurrant, strawberry, raspberry, and some varieties of gooseberries and hybrid berries from nurserymen who should be able to supply the certificate number given to the stock by the Ministry of Agriculture. Plants that are obviously infected with virus disease should be pulled up and burned. This is particularly worthwhile in the first year of a bed, when the infected plant can easily be replaced by a healthy one.

The only way of ensuring that plants are of first-grade quality is by making purchases from a nurseryman recommended by *Which* (published by the Consumers Association), from a nurseryman who guarantees to replace any plants that die, or from a nurseryman who experience has shown sells good-quality plants.

Importance of Correct Handling of Plants

When plants are received, the ideal would be to plant them immediately if the soil has been prepared and it is in plantable condition; that is, dry enough to be firmed without turning into a sticky mess. Otherwise, heel the plants into a trench, having untied the bundles, spaced out the roots and lightly covered them with damp soil. If the soil is frozen, open the package and make sure that the roots have not dried out, moisten them if necessary and then re-close the package and store it in a cold shed until the soil thaws out.

Time of Planting

Fruit bushes, but not strawberries, may be planted at any time during the winter while they are dormant, but growth will be better if they are planted before Christmas. Bushes should be ordered early in the autumn from a nurseryman with the stipulation that they should be delivered before the end of November. They should be planted as soon as the soil is dry enough and can be worked into a tilth, so that the soil can be firmed over the roots without forming a sticky mess.

The distances between the rows of bushes should be 5 or 6 ft for all kinds of fruit except strawberries. Modern vigorous varieties really require to be planted at the wider distance and should only be planted 5 ft apart when the size of the garden makes the wider distance impossible.

Fruit Plot Management

All fruits grow more satisfactorily and produce the heaviest crops in soil that is undisturbed in any way by cultivation and therefore wherever possible weeds should be controlled by the application of weedkiller. Fortunately all the soft fruits (with the exception of strawberries) are remarkably tolerant to Weedex (simazine). Gardeners who are prepared carefully to carry out the application instructions should, whenever they can, use Weedex in their crops as it is most effective in preventing the growth of annual weeds.

The following instructions should and must be followed:

1. The time of application should be February in the south and March in the north of the country.
2. The soil should be free of all weeds at time of application.
3. The soil should be moist, have a fine firm tilth and not be cloddy.
4. Under certain conditions cleavers, knotgrass and redshank may not be prevented from germinating by Weedex. When this occurs these weeds should be killed by Dutch hoeing and not allowed to seed.
5. If the soil was not completely cleared of perennial weeds before planting they will flourish and overrun the plot in the absence of competition from other weeds and cultivation. They should be dealt with by applying by hand with a brush a ten per cent solution of Fison's Tumbleweed.
6. Under normal conditions in the autumn after the first application of Weedex, moss will grow on the soil. It should be allowed to flourish and form a complete carpet; it is not harmful to the bushes and makes an excellent surface on which to walk.

Method of Application

1. After planting, rake and tread the soil into a level fine tilth and at the same time form a ridge of soil 2 in. high over the roots of the canes or bushes.
2. The Weedex should be applied with a spraying machine or watering can.
3. (a) *Light soils* – mix one sachet in 2 gallons of water and apply to 50 square yards.
   (b) *Heavy soils* – mix one sachet in 2 gallons of water and apply to 33 square yards.
4. Around established bushes make similar applications without disturbing the soil in any way. If any annual soft weeds are present these may be killed by spraying with Weedol.
5. Casoron G may be applied to control docks, mare's tail, perennial nettle and thistles. The granules should be sprinkled over the weed-infested areas during February at the rate of $\frac{1}{3}$ oz. to each square yard.

Weed Control in Strawberries

Only Covershield should be applied to strawberries *immediately after planting* at the rate of 1 oz. to 7·5 square yards. This application should prevent weeds from germinating for six weeks, when a second application should be made. Strawberries are less resistant to applications of Weedex.

At the end of August, when the plants are growing strongly and have produced a minimum of four fully developed leaves, applications of Weedex may commence provided the soil has a fine moist tilth and is free from weeds.
There is a choice of

1. One application each year in August:
   Light soils – one sachet in 2 gallons of water to 50 square yards.
   Heavy soils – one sachet in 2 gallons of water to 33 square yards.
2. Two applications each year, one in August and the other in November:
   Light soils – one sachet in 2 gallons of water to 100 square yards.
   Heavy soils – one sachet in 2 gallons of water to 66 square yards.

The two-application method is the better one as it is safer and more effective.
Weedex should not be applied to very light sandy or gravelly soils.

Pests and Diseases

As it is easier to prevent than cure a severe infestation a constant look out should be kept for the troubles that reduce the yields of fruit. To achieve this aim an efficient spraying machine should be purchased so that all parts of the plant can be sprayed with chemical. If the chemicals are to be effective they should be mixed with water at the exact rate recommended by the manufacturer.

The pests and diseases that cause trouble on all these soft fruits are:

Botrytis Fruit Rot or Grey Mould

This disease first infects the dying petals and stamens and later spreads to the developing fruits and causes them to rot. It is important to realise that precautions must begin at **flowering time** and that all the flowering parts should be covered with fungicide.

Spray with Benlate or Systemic fungicide when the first flowers are opening followed by two further applications at fourteen day intervals. The final application applies to strawberries only.

Cane Spot

This disease only infects the cane fruits and can be particularly serious on loganberries and the raspberry varieties Malling Jewel and Leo. Round purple spots will be found on the new canes and leaves from June onwards. Later the spots elongate and their centres turn white. Serious infections reduce yields and kill the canes.

To control cane spot: The sprays applied for Botrytis fruit rot should be extended to cover the new canes.

Botrytis grey mould infecting strawberry fruits

Healthy and big bud mite infested blackcurrant buds

Healthy and greenfly infested blackcurrant shoo

*Powdery mildew on gooseberry (above)
and on blackcurrant shoot (below)*

Raspberry beetle larva

Green Capsid Bug

The small bright green insect is similar to but differs from greenfly by running very quickly over the leaves. It feeds in the growing points of the shoots, causing them to become stunted and branched, and gives rise to characteristic holes in leaves and cat-faced fruits in strawberries.

As soon as the brown feeding marks are seen on the leaves in early May, spray the tips of the shoots and the crowns of strawberries with Fenitrothion.

Greenfly (Aphids)

These plant lice infest all the soft-fruit plants, can cause serious damage to strawberries, black currants and gooseberries, but are less serious on raspberries and cane fruits. They are also responsible for infecting plants with many of the virus diseases. The worst infestations usually develop in the spring and should be dealt with before they become serious by spraying with Fenitrothion or Malathion. Where a bad infestation has occurred and the leaves have curled up, spray with Systemic insecticide.

Big Bud Mite

This is a microscopic insect that feeds inside blackcurrant buds, causing them to swell to the size of peas and fail to open. More seriously, they can infect the bushes with reversion virus. Picking off and burning swollen buds is only partially successful in controlling this pest as there will be small numbers of mites inside what appear to be normal buds. Spraying with Benlate three times during May and June gives partial control of big bud mite.

9

Leaf Spot

This disease infects all the currant and gooseberry varieties. From April onwards angular brown spots appear on the leaves, and if allowed to develop unchecked will cover all the leaves and cause them to drop off by the time the fruit is ripe. Not only does the disease reduce the current crop but it will reduce that of the following year.

Leaf spot is controlled by fungicides applied for Botrytis fruit rot control or by applications of Dithane 945.

Powdery Mildew

Mildew infects blackcurrants, gooseberries, raspberries and strawberries. The stems and leaves become covered with a characteristic white mycelium which cripples the growth of the plants. The fruits also become infected and in severe cases are inedible.

Effective control depends upon making an early application of fungicide in early May, followed by at least two further applications at three-weekly intervals. The most effective chemical is Nimrod T.

Raspberry Beetle

The small brown beetle can be found feeding on raspberries, black and hybrid berries from mid May until mid July. First it feeds on the buds and flowers, causing malformed berries. Later it lays eggs that hatch out into white grubs that will be present in the ripe berries.

Spray and thoroughly wet the berries with Fenitrothion or Malathion as the first fruits turn colour.

Raspberry Leaf and Bud Mite

This mite overwinters under the bud scales and in spring migrates to the new leaves and developing fruits. The feeding areas turn yellow and are difficult to distinguish from symptoms of virus infection. The fruit is crumbly, yield is reduced and canes are stunted. No insecticide is available to the amateur gardener for use against this pest.

Raspberry Midge Blight

The fruiting canes either fail to leaf out in the spring or wilt and die during the spring and summer. The trouble emanates from the previous summer when raspberry cane midges laid eggs under the bark of the new canes at the end of May and beginning of June.

The larvae that hatched out enabled various fungal diseases to infect the canes.

To prevent a recurrence of the trouble next year, the new canes should be thoroughly wetted with a spray of Fenitrothion during the last days of May and again ten days later.

Red Spider Mite

This serious pest may infest any of the soft fruits, causing serious reductions in growth and yield. The bright red overwintering mites move from shelter to the new foliage. There they live on the undersides of the leaves and suck the sap. At the start of an attack, the feeding marks can be distinguished as minute white spots on the upper surfaces of the leaves. If the attack is not checked, the spots merge and the leaves turn brown and become useless to the plant.

Spray the bushes with Dimethoate or Sybol 2, thoroughly wetting the undersurfaces of the leaves.

Spur Blight and Botrytis of the Canes

Infection with these diseases occurs from July onwards when purple coloured blotches appear on the new canes. In extreme cases whole lengths of cane can be affected. Later the infected areas turn silvery white in colour and exhibit black spots – the fruiting bodies of the diseases. The canes may die or the buds may fail to grow out.

These diseases are worse where bushes are growing too strongly due to excess application of nitrogenous fertiliser or where an excessive number of canes have been allowed to grow in the row. The sprays for the control of Botrytis fruit rot, if extended to cover the new canes, will control these diseases.

Reversion of Blackcurrant

Branches or whole bushes will suddenly not bear any fruit. If other bushes are bearing fruit it is reasonable to assume the bushes are infected with reversion virus. This should be confirmed by examining the leaves, which have a coarse appearance with few veins and a small number of large serrations. The only cure is to dig up and burn diseased bushes before they infect healthy ones.

Raspberry leaf and bud mite infested leaves

Raspberry canes attacked by midge blight

Healthy and reverted blackcurrant leaves

Raspberry spur blight

Types and Varieties

GOOSEBERRIES, RED AND WHITE CURRANTS

Gooseberries and currants flower early in the spring but, because they have resistance to spring frosts, well-managed bushes can usually be relied upon to bear heavy crops.

Gooseberry Varieties

Careless – this is the most popular variety as it crops well and is easy to grow. Picked for bottling, jam making and pies it is dark green, but turns greenish white when fully ripe.

Invicta – a new very vigorous and thorny variety. Its chief merits are heavy yields and resistance to mildew.

Whinhams Industry – a green variety for cooking but turns red when ripe and can be eaten for dessert.

Leveller – this variety, when ripe, has the reputation of being the gooseberry with the most flavour. As it is difficult to grow it should only be grown to produce ripe fruit for eating raw.

Captivator – a thornless variety that bears a large number of small red berries.

Careless   *Whinhams Industry*

Above: Jonkheer van Tets. Below: White Versailles

Currant Varieties

Jonkheer van Tets – this is a red Dutch variety that ripens its fruit early towards the end of July.

Redstart – a new variety that outyields all other varieties; the fruit makes a very good red-currant jelly. The bush is moderately vigorous, erect and fairly resistant to wind damage.

White Versailles – a variety the fruit of which is pale green or almost white in colour.

13

Planting Stock

Certified stocks of gooseberries are only now becoming available, and it should be possible to purchase virus-tested Jubilee (synonym Careless) and Invicta.

Gooseberries and currants are sold as two- and three-year bushes and provided the two-year bushes are well grown these are the best and cheapest buy. Such a bush should have a straight clean leg 10 in. long and a minimum of three branches each 15 in. in length equally spaced round the stem. A three-year-old should have six branches and a number of fruiting spurs.

Planting Distances

5–6 ft between rows. 4–5 ft between the bushes. They may also be planted and trained as single or double cordons on wires against a wall or free-standing on posts and wires. Plant single cordons 12 in. apart and double cordons 30 in. apart.

Planting

Before planting carefully examine the stems and cut off any buds that are present as these will later grow into unwanted suckers. Plant with 3–4 in. of the stem below soil level. Any roots that remain exposed should be cut off.

Manuring

In March, after planting, broadcast on the soil in a circle 18 in. in diameter round each bush ½ oz. of nitro-chalk and ½ oz. of sulphate of potash. Each March in the following years broadcast on the soil, 3 ft either side of the bushes, ⅓ oz. of nitro-chalk and ½ oz. of sulphate of potash. The object of applying nitrogenous fertiliser is to obtain 12–18 in. of new growth each year. If the bushes do not make this growth increase the amount of nitro-chalk; if there is too much growth reduce the amount.

Spread roots out in planting hole, firm well and, for gooseberry and redcurrant, leave 10 inches of stem above the soil

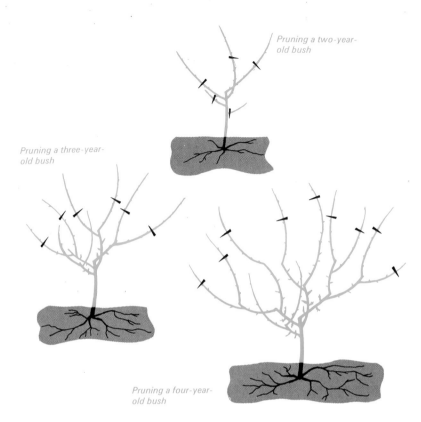

Pruning a two-year-old bush

Pruning a three-year-old bush

Pruning a four-year-old bush

Pruning

Unless grown in a fruit cage prune the bushes in March. The objective is to grow a cup-shaped bush with the branches spaced equally round the circumference. The number of branches should be increased by cutting the leading shoots back to left- and right-hand facing buds. When there are sufficient branches, prune the leading shoots to upward-facing buds to prevent the branches from drooping. The formation of a well-shaped bush should be hastened by rubbing out in June and July any new shoots that are growing in the wrong directions, and by summer pruning all lateral shoots to leave five leaves at the end of July. Any suckers that grow from below the soil or on the main stem should be pulled off while their wood is still soft.

Picking

Gooseberries should be picked over a period of several weeks starting as early as Whitsun and ending in early August. Each time only the largest berries are picked and the penultimate picking in early July should leave berries spaced 2 in. apart. These should be left to grow very large and fully ripe for eating as dessert fruit.

Red currants are picked as they ripen over a fairly short period of time towards the end of July.

BLACKCURRANTS

The traditional varieties are no longer worth growing because they have been outdated by heavier yielding varieties that are resistant to spring frost damage.

Tenah – the earliest variety but its potential high yield is reduced by the necessity to prune severely its straggling branches unless the branches are supported. In a garden the branches of the bush could be tied around with string.

Ben Lomond – a mid-season variety that crops very heavily. The bushes are upright, compact, mildew-resistant and require very little pruning. The berries are large.

Ben More – another mid-season variety. It is a very vigorous upright grower that is immune to mildew. The berries are very large.

Ben Sarek – a new variety bred specifically for garden use. The bushes are small in size and very heavy yielding. The fruit ripens a few days earlier than that of Ben Lomond.

Malling Jet – late ripening towards the end of August. It is easy to pick as each string carries as many as eighteen medium-sized berries.

Types of Planting Material

1. One-year-old bushes are good value for money provided they have a MAFF certificate. They should have a minimum of two branches 18 in. long.

2. Two-year-old bushes should have between three and five branches 24 in. in length. They are more expensive to buy but produce a full crop more quickly.

3. Three-year-old bushes. Although good specimens have five branches or more they are not worth buying because transplanting a bush of this age is too large a check to growth.

Planting

5–6 ft between the rows 2½ or 5 ft between the bushes. The closer planting distance gives double the yield of fruit than the wider spacing in the first three to four years. The bushes should be planted 2–3 in. deeper than in the nursery. so that the soil is level with the place where the branches divide.

Ben Lomond *Ben Sarek*

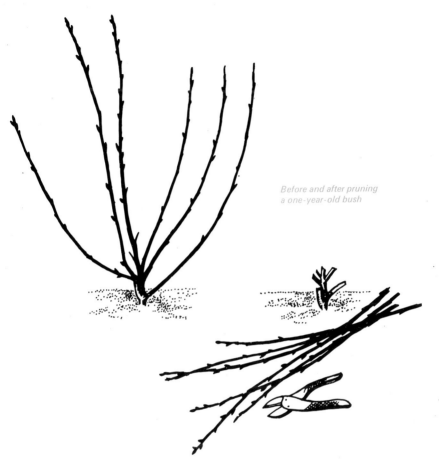

*Before and after pruning
a one-year-old bush*

Pruning

Immediately after planting cut each branch back so that two buds remain above soil level. At the end of the first year's growth cut out any weak, thin shoots and one strong branch in each bush. This is to encourage new strong basal shoots in the following year. On fully grown bushes cut off at their bases all branches that are growing out at an angle of less than 45° from the horizontal.

Each year the heights of five-year and older bushes should be reduced by cutting back three or four branches to new shoots.

Manuring

After planting at the end of March broadcast, in a circle 18 in. in diameter round each bush, 1 oz. of nitro-chalk and $\frac{1}{2}$ oz. of sulphate of potash. At the end of May similarly broadcast $\frac{1}{2}$ oz. of nitrochalk. In every March following broadcast over the soil 3 ft either side of the row of bushes $\frac{1}{2}$ oz. of nitro-chalk and $\frac{1}{2}$ oz. of sulphate of potash per square yard.

RASPBERRIES

Summer Varieties

Glen Clova – an early heavy-cropping variety that grows vigorously. It is very susceptible to 'die back' caused by midge blight. Fruits are of good quality.

Delight – another early variety that crops heavily. The berries are very large and thin skinned. Aphid-resistant.

Malling Jewel – a mid-season variety that is easy to grow and tolerant of virus infections. The yield is moderate and the fruits are of good flavour and quality.

Malling Admiral – the fruits are large, conical in shape and of excellent flavour. The yield is moderate. Aphid-resistant.

Leo – the latest-ripening variety, bearing moderate crops of good-quality fruit. The canes are prickly. Aphid-resistant.

Joy – a new late-ripening variety that crops very heavily, but the canes and fruit stalks are very prickly. Aphid-resistant.

Glen Moy – a new heavy-yielding early variety that is resistant to aphid infestation. The fruits are of good quality. The canes are spine-free.

Glen Prosen – a mid- to late-season variety, probably not as heavy yielding as Glen Moy. The fruits are particularly firm and of good quality. The canes are spineless and aphid-resistant.

Autumn Varieties

Bliss – a new autumn-fruiting variety, stocks of which will be available in autumn 1985. It is large-fruited and heavy yielding because the fruits ripen from early August.

Zeva – this is an autumn-fruiting variety that bears fruit on the tips of the current season's new canes. The picking season is prolonged – from mid September until November – and the yield is low compared with summer varieties. The best-flavoured autumn-fruiting variety.

Glen Clova

Malling Delight

Malling Admiral
Glen Moy

Joy
Glen Prosen

Fallgold

Zeva

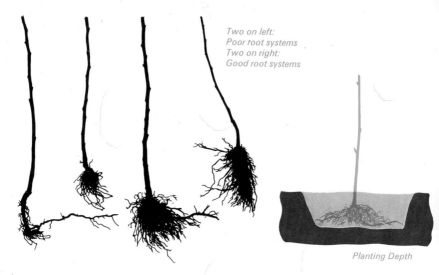

Two on left:
Poor root systems
Two on right:
Good root systems

Planting Depth

RASPBERRY TRAINING (Scottish Stool Method)

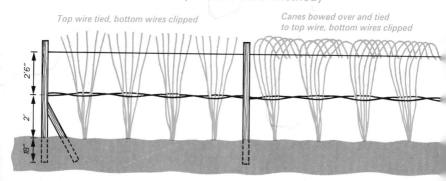

Top wire tied, bottom wires clipped

Canes bowed over and tied
to top wire, bottom wires clipped

2'6"

2'

18"

Detail of tying

Details of canes bowed over

Planting Stock
It is important that only certified canes of good physical quality should be planted. Canes should be judged by the presence of a good fibrous root system and not by the thickness or length of the cane.

Soil
Raspberries do not thrive on very heavy or poorly drained soils. They do best on deep gritty soils that are well drained.

Isolating the Roots
Raspberries can be a nuisance because their roots spread for many yards and throw up suckers among other fruit crops and outside the fruit plot. The only effective way of preventing this is to dig a narrow trench across the ends of and 3 ft from the raspberry row, to a depth of 2–3 ft. Bury vertically sheets of thick polythene, asbestos or corrugated iron in the trench and then replace the soil.

Planting
5 or 6 ft between the rows and 24 in. between the plants in the rows. In the case of Malling Jewel and Leo place two canes together at each planting position. Raspberries should not be planted too deep but so that the white buds are just below the soil surface.

The canes should be cut back to 12 in. in length before planting.

Manuring
At the end of March broadcast on the soil in a circle 18 in. in diameter round each bush 1 oz. of nitro-chalk and $\frac{1}{2}$ oz. of sulphate of potash. Similarly at the end of May and the end of June broadcast $\frac{2}{3}$ oz. of nitro-chalk. At the end of March in the years following broadcast 3 ft either side of the rows $\frac{1}{3}$ oz. of nitro-chalk and $\frac{1}{2}$ oz. of sulphate of potash per square yard. If the canes grow too tall the nitrogen application should be omitted.

Post and wire supports
Posts and wires should be erected in November after planting and the canes secured to the wires. The posts should measure 2 in. × 3 in. × 6 ft 6 in. long and be driven into the soil to a depth of 18 in. The posts should be positioned 10 yards maximum apart and the end posts should be strutted. Three strands of 13 gauge galvanised wire should be stapled to the posts – a single top wire to which the individual canes are tied and a pair of wires at half the cane height between which the canes are clipped (see diagram opposite).

Winter and Summer Pruning
Pruning may be carried out at any time during the winter. It consists of cutting out the spent fruiting canes at their bases together with any new canes that are weak or damaged so that a maximum of eight strong new canes remain on each stool to be tied to the wires. After tying in, the canes are tipped at a height of 5 ft 6 in. so that the fruit can be picked easily. The tips should also be removed from bowed-over canes.

Summer pruning consists of the routine hoeing off or pulling out of all new suckers that grow away from the main stools. They should be removed before they exceed a height of 6 in. This operation should be done in early May, in June and again before picking.

BLACK AND HYBRID BERRIES

The weights of crop that these fruits bear are related to the lengths of season over which they ripen their berries. Ripening can be brought to a premature end by an early autumn frost in September or October. An early-ripening variety usually has the highest yield. Late-ripening varieties are not worth growing in northern parts of the United Kingdom.

Varieties

Tayberry – this is a new loganberry-type cross that crops more heavily and has berries that are half as large again. The berries are less acid and have more flavour. The canes are spiny.

Loganberry LY654 – considered to be a cross between a wild blackberry and a red raspberry. The berries are very large and ripen in July/August. The advantage of this clone is that it is thornless.

Sunberry – the fruits are similar to those of the loganberry but they are partially hidden by the leaves. The plant is very vigorous with thorny canes.

Thornless Boysenberry – the berries are very large and purplish black in colour with a good and not too acid flavour. Ripens about ten days later than the loganberry (July/August). Drought-resistant.

Bedford Giant – a reliable heavy cropper with large black berries that have a weak flavour. The canes are vigorous and thorny. The earliest variety.

Himalayan Giant – has very vigorous canes with massive thorns. The jet-black berries have a moderate flavour. Heavy cropper.

Ashton Cross – produces a very heavy crop of medium-sized well-flavoured berries. The canes are thin and thorny.

Oregon Thornless – besides being thornless, the advantages of this variety are that the foliage is parsley leaved and therefore very decorative, the plant is not rampant and the quality and flavour of the berries is particularly good. Moderate cropper. Late ripening.

Smoothstem – a heavy-yielding late variety with thornless stems.

Tayberry

Thornless Loganberry LY654

Oregon Thornless
Thornless Boysenberry

Ashton Cross

Planting Stock

Very few certified stocks of these kinds of fruit have been available for purchase. In the future, Ministry of Agriculture Certified Stocks should become available.

Types of Planting Material

1. The best type to plant is a one-year plant that should have two or more cut-back shoots and a strong root system.

2. One-year canes that are similar to a raspberry cane, which have grown at least 4 ft in the nursery and have a large root system.

3. Rooted cuttings or tips in pots, though small, are satisfactory but take longer to come to full bearing.

Planting

Bare-root plants should be planted during the winter; plants growing in pots may be planted at any time, but will probably require watering if planted when in leaf. They may be planted against a wall or a fence but the fruit will be later ripening on a north-facing wall and earlier on a south-facing one. When grown in the open they must be supported on a framework of strong posts and wires.

Planting Distances

6 ft is the minimum distance these fruits require between the rows; an extra foot makes them easier to manage.

Distances in the rows are as follows

Ashton Cross	12 ft	**Tayberry**	8 ft
Bedford Giant	12 ft	**Thornless Boysenberry**	8 ft
Oregon Thornless	6 ft	**Thornless Loganberry**	8 ft
Sunberry	15 ft	**Himalayan Giant**	15 ft

CROPPING PERIODS

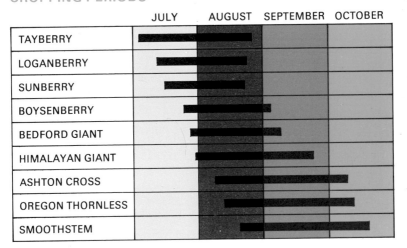

	JULY	AUGUST	SEPTEMBER	OCTOBER
TAYBERRY				
LOGANBERRY				
SUNBERRY				
BOYSENBERRY				
BEDFORD GIANT				
HIMALAYAN GIANT				
ASHTON CROSS				
OREGON THORNLESS				
SMOOTHSTEM				

Blackberry picking

25

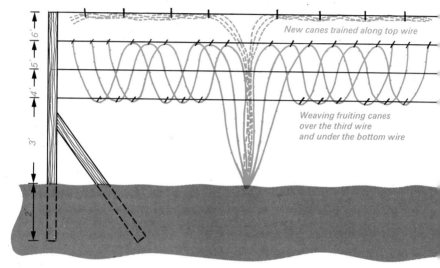

New canes trained along top wire

Weaving fruiting canes
over the third wire
and under the bottom wire

Post and wire supports

4 in.×4 in. posts, 8 ft long, should be driven into the ground to a depth of 2 ft. Intermediate posts of 3 in.×3 in. thickness should be positioned every 25 ft along the row. The end posts should be supported by straining posts.

No. 11 gauge galvanised wire should be stretched along the posts at heights of 3, 4, 5 and 6 ft (see diagram above).

Training

In the first year after planting the new canes should be woven over the third wire and under the bottom wire as they grow, tying them in place as necessary. In this position they bear their fruit the following year.

During the second year the new canes as they grow should be tied vertically in a bunch to the lower wires until they reach the top wire. They are then divided into two lots and trained opposite ways along the top wire.

In succeeding years (in March) the canes that have fruited should be cut back to their bases and removed from the wires. The new canes are taken down from the top wire and woven up and over the bottom wires as shown in the diagram.

Manuring

After planting at the end of March broadcast in a circle 18 in. in diameter round each plant 1 oz. of nitro-chalk and $\frac{1}{2}$ oz. of sulphate of potash. At the end of May and at the beginning of July broadcast in a circle 36 in. in diameter 1 oz. of nitro-chalk.

In succeeding years (in March) broadcast over the soil 3 ft either side of the row $\frac{1}{2}$ oz. of nitro-chalk and $\frac{1}{2}$ oz. of sulphate of potash. The application of nitrogen may have to be increased or decreased if there is too little or too great a length of cane respectively to furnish the wires fully.

STRAWBERRIES

There are approximately sixty strawberry varieties available for purchase in this country but only a small number are available as certified plants and considered to be suitable for growing in private gardens.

Early Varieties

Pantagruella – bears a moderate crop of medium to small fruits. It should be planted 9 in. apart in the row. Flowers are liable to be killed by frost in low-lying situations. The berries ripen very early and are of good flavour.

Redgauntlet – this is a heavy-cropping variety that bears medium to large bright red fruits. In the south of the country it bears a second crop in the autumn. The flavour is satisfactory provided the fruit is eaten with sugar and cream.

Pantagruella

Mid-season Varieties

Cambridge Favourite – most widely grown because it can be relied on to crop well in all situations. The berries 'hang' on the plants for a long period without going rotten or getting over-ripe. Its chief trouble is infestation by red spider mite.

Hapil – a recently introduced variety that crops well and has a much better flavour than Favourite. Very large fruits; drought-resistant; heavy cropping.

Maxim – the newest variety for the private garden. The fruits are very large and of good flavour and quality. Very free cropper. (See front cover.)

Tamella – a very heavy-cropping variety that picks over an extended period. The primary fruits are very large but, as they are soft, require very careful picking. The flavour is good.

Totem – this is a red-fleshed variety that should be grown primarily for freezing. It retains its shape and flavour and does not lose its juice after thawing. Moderate cropper.

Cambridge Favourite

Tamella

Hapil

Domanil

Tenira

Late Mid-season Varieties

Domanil – this is the latest-ripening variety available. Large berries of good flavour.
Tenira – given good growing conditions and adequate moisture this variety bears heavy crops of extremely well-flavoured fruit.

Planting Stock

Whenever possible purchase certified runners or plants. Three types of plants are available:

1. **September to April** – freshly dug open-ground runners.
2. **May to August** – open-ground runners that have had the leaves cut off and have been kept in refrigerated storage until required for planting. They must be thoroughly watered-in after planting.
3. **All year round** – runners that have been grown on in Jiffy 7s or in pots of compost. In dry weather these also require watering after planting.

Planting

Strawberries should not be planted out-doors between mid November and mid February (mid October and end of March in the north). Plants should be examined immediately they are received and whatever their condition of dryness should be immersed in water for five minutes. If they cannot be planted immediately they should be heeled-in in moist soil in a shady place.

The soil in which the strawberries are to be planted should have been dug some time previously. Broadcast over it $\frac{1}{2}$ oz. of nitro-chalk and $\frac{1}{2}$ oz. of sulphate of potash. The soil should then be raked and rolled until it is as firm as a seedbed prepared for sowing small seeds. Planting distances should be 30–36 in. between the rows and 12–15 in. between the plants. It is extremely important that strawberries should be planted firmly and at the correct depth. If the roots are too long they should be shortened to 4 in. with a knife. After planting, the base of the crown should be sitting at soil level (see illustration). If the crown is buried or the roots are exposed the plants will not thrive and may eventually die.

Centre runner planted correctly

Cutting stolons on maiden strawberry plant

De-blossoming

Flowers will appear on newly planted runners in May or in the case of cold-stored runners, one month after planting. Provided the plants are growing strongly, they may be left to produce fruit. If for any reason growth is not satisfactory, the flower trusses should be cut off with scissors. This enables the plants to devote their resoures to building up new crowns that produce the following year's crop.

Treatment of the New Runners

From June onwards, stolons and runners will grow from the crowns and the decision should be made whether to have a bed of single plants or of matted rows. Single plants are easier to keep free from weeds, the fruit is well displayed for picking but the yield of fruit will be lower. To maintain single plants the stolons should be systematically cut off as soon as they are 3 or 4 in. long.

To form a matted row, the new runners as they develop should be trained to root into the strip of soil 15–18 in. wide on either side of the row of parent plants. For each parent plant between six and nine runners should be allowed to root. Runners that appear in excess of these numbers should be cut off so that clear pathways 15–18 in. wide remain for walking on. A bed of matted rows should produce thirty to forty per cent more fruit than a bed of single plants.

Manuring during the cropping years

A healthy well-established strawberry bed requires very little fertiliser $-\frac{1}{2}$ oz. of sulphate of potash per square yard applied each March. Only if the plants fail to make satisfactory growth, the leaves being small and pale in colour, should it be necessary to apply $\frac{1}{3}$ to $\frac{2}{3}$ oz. of nitro-chalk to each square yard.

Strawing

At the beginning of June straw should be spread along the rows and tucked under the fruit trusses. This keeps the fruit free from soil and provides a clean walking surface. A ½ cwt bale of straw will cover 80 square yards of bed.

Summer Cleaning After Picking

Immediately after picking, the bed should be thoroughly weeded. At the same time all the leaves should be cut off with a pair of shears. On no account should this operation be delayed or the next year's crop will be reduced instead of increased. Afterwards a new set of leaves appears, to manufacture food that is used to form next year's flower buds.

Strawberries growing in Tower Pots